COLORING CHECKLIST

- ☐ BEACHY VIBES
- ☐ ROLLIN' AROUND
- ☐ STARRY SKIES
- ☐ BBQ BASH
- ☐ GONE FISHIN'
- ☐ SHADES OF SUMMER
- ☐ COUNTY FAIR
- ☐ UNDER THE SEA
- ☐ CHILLY TREATS
- ☐ GAME DAY
- ☐ POOL PARTY
- ☐ PICNIC AT THE PARK
- ☐ SUMMER WARDROBE
- ☐ CAMPFIRE FUN
- ☐ TROPICAL PARADISE
- ☐ BOATING ADVENTURES
- ☐ KITE FLYING FRENZY
- ☐ ROAD TRIPPIN'
- ☐ GARDENING OASIS
- ☐ ICE CREAM SUNDAE
- ☐ WATERPARK SPLASH
- ☐ NATURE HIKES
- ☐ FRESH FRUIT
- ☐ THEME PARK THRILLS
- ☐ MOVIE MARATHON
- ☐ SUNNY SANDALS
- ☐ SUMMER BUGS
- ☐ DAY AT THE ZOO
- ☐ ICY REFRESHMENTS
- ☐ BACKYARD WATER FUN
- ☐ CREATIVE CORNER
- ☐ SIDEWALK CHALK

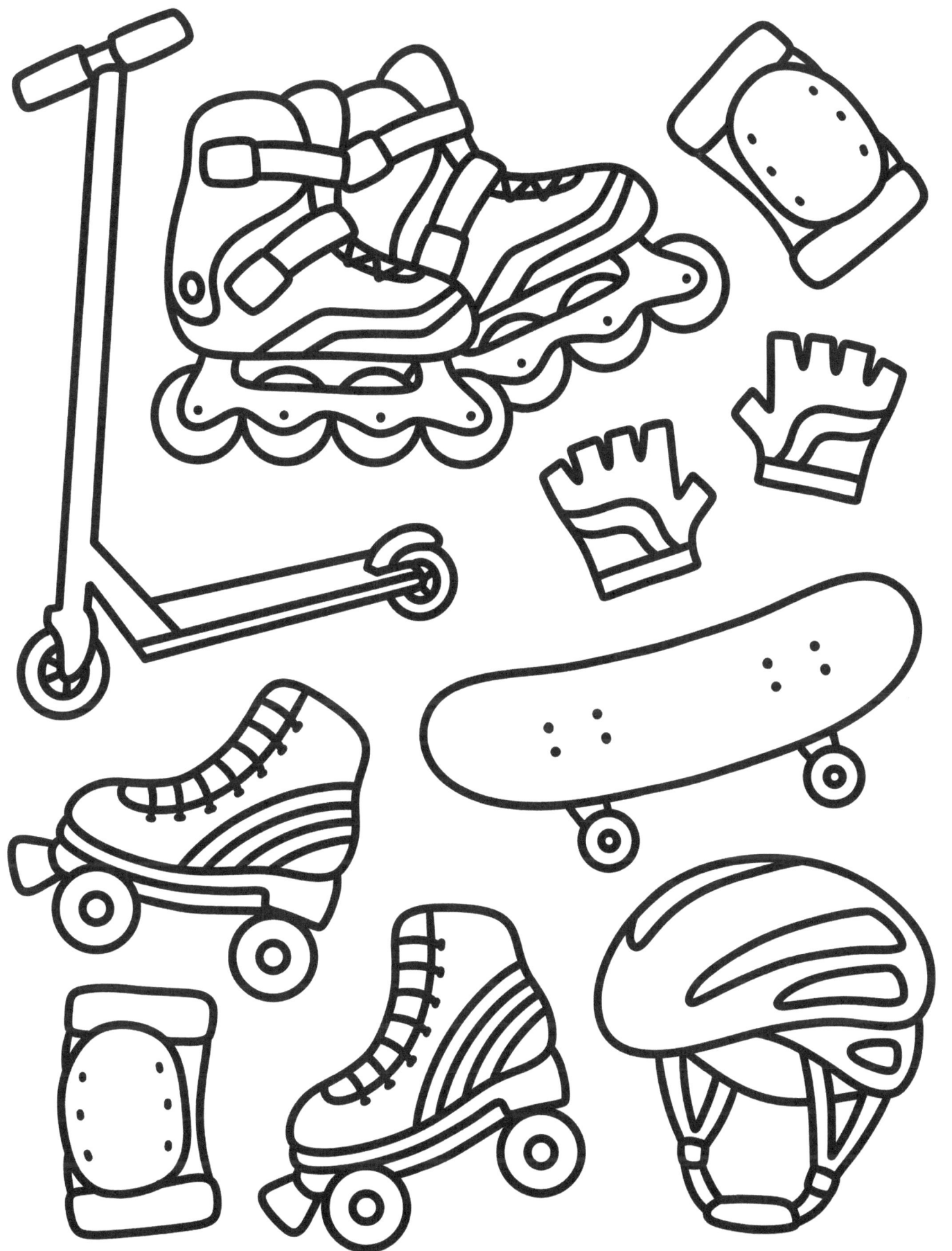

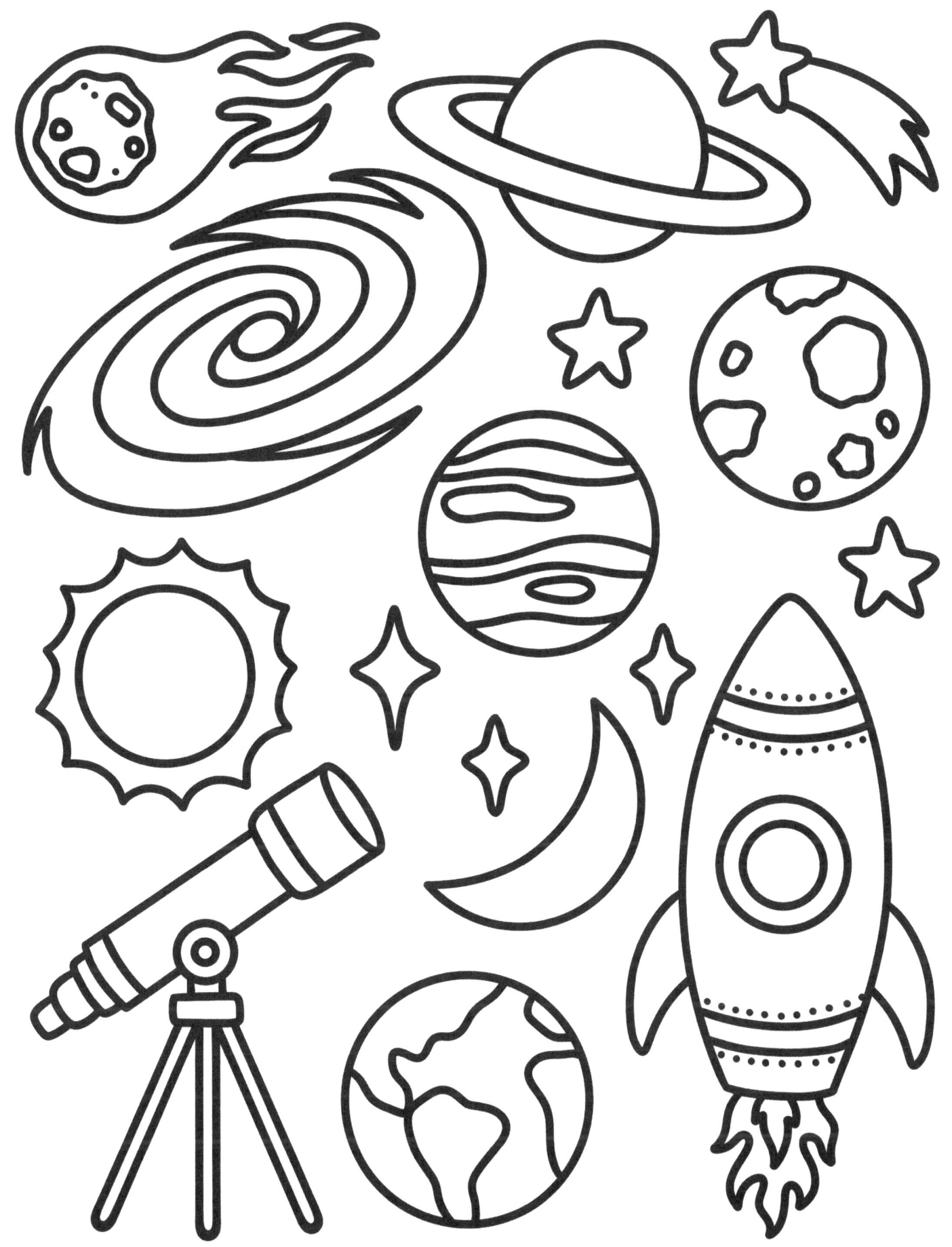

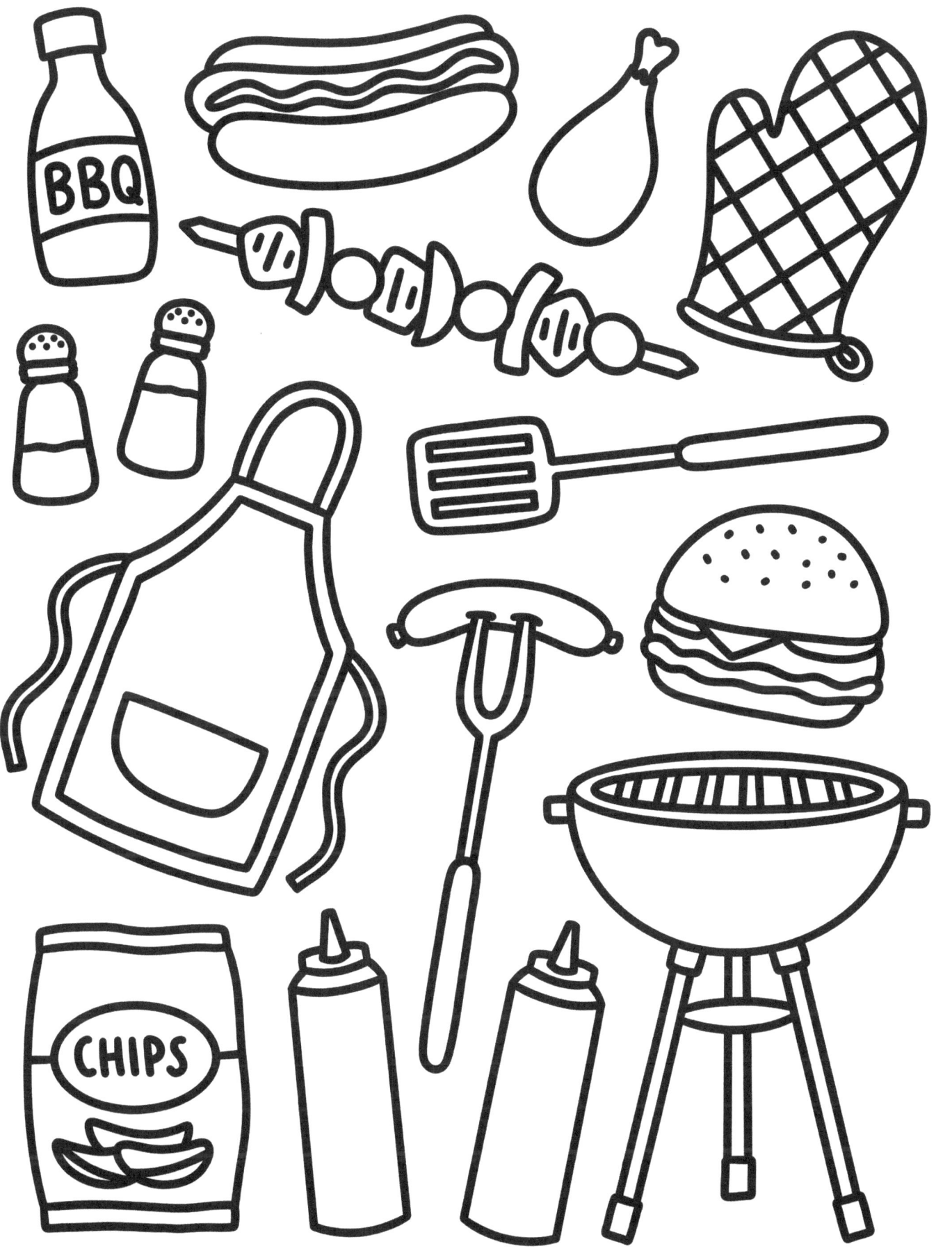

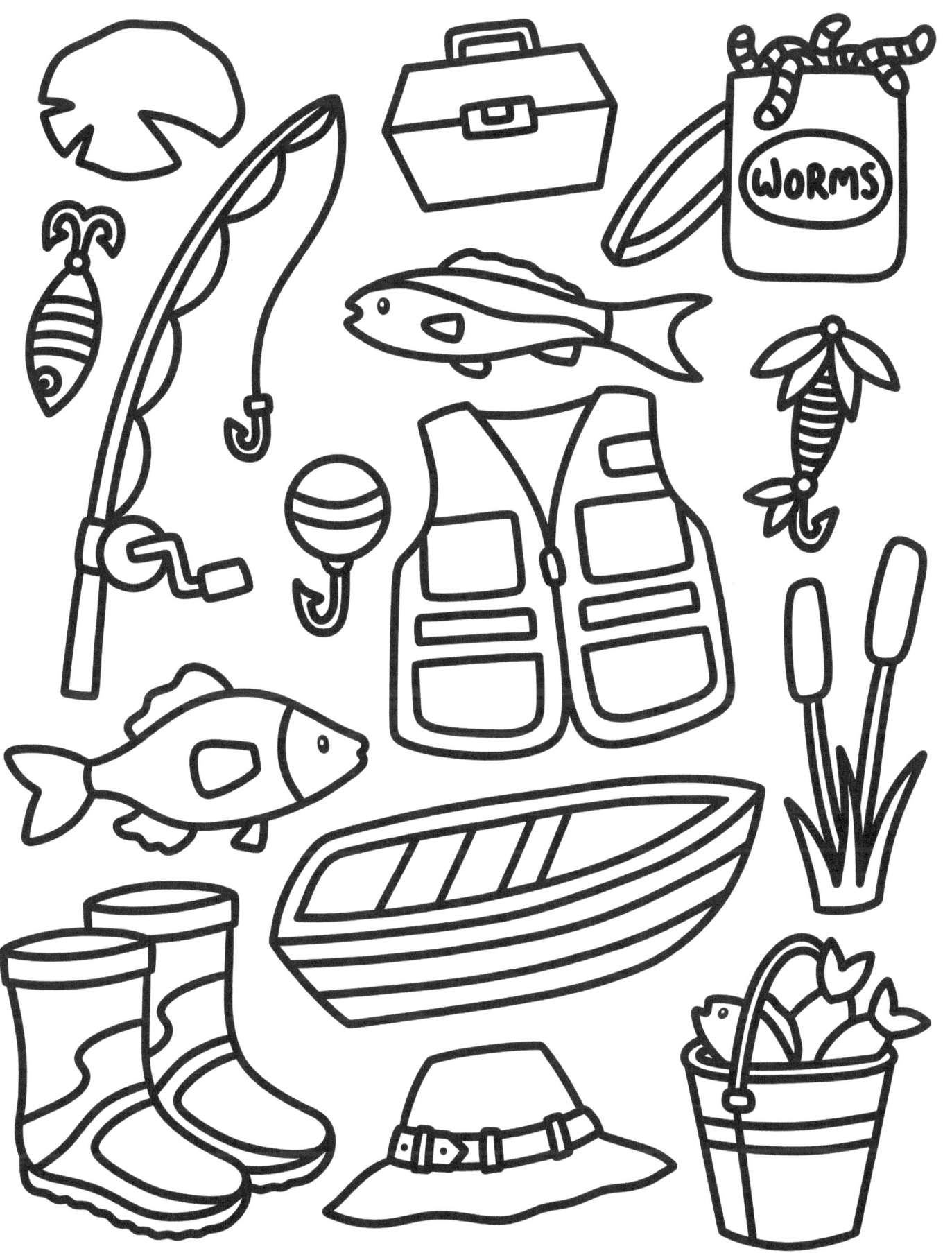

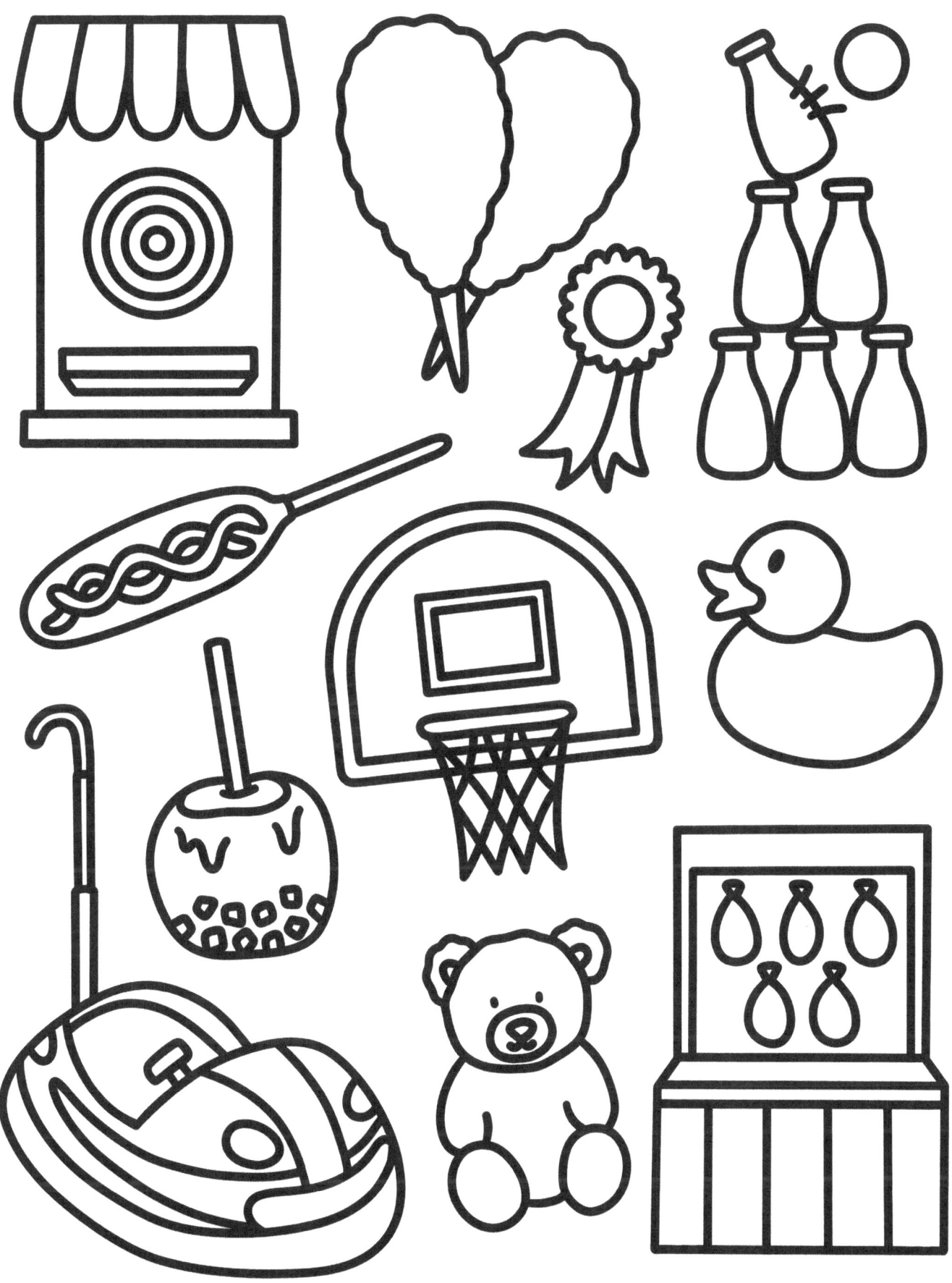

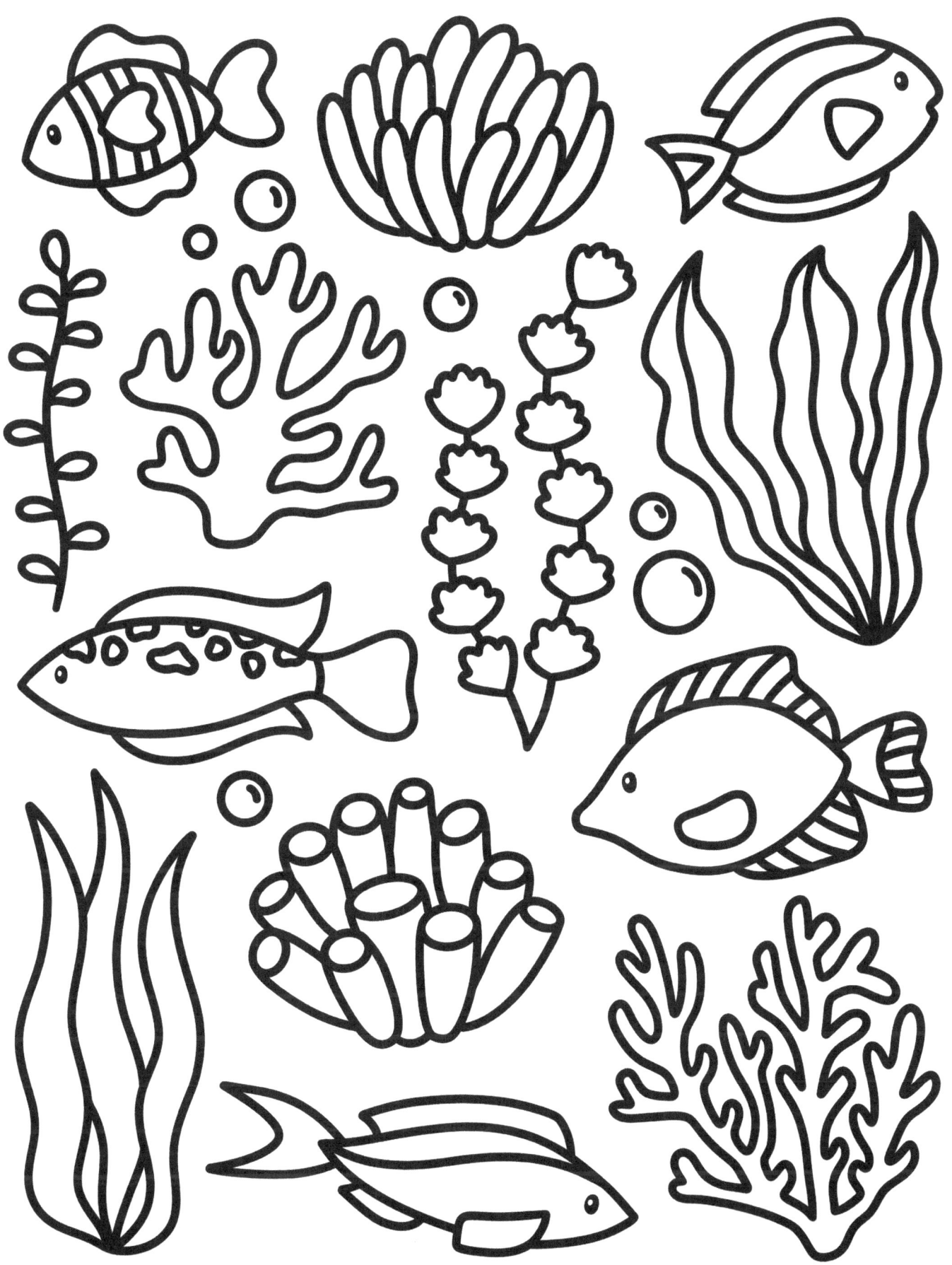

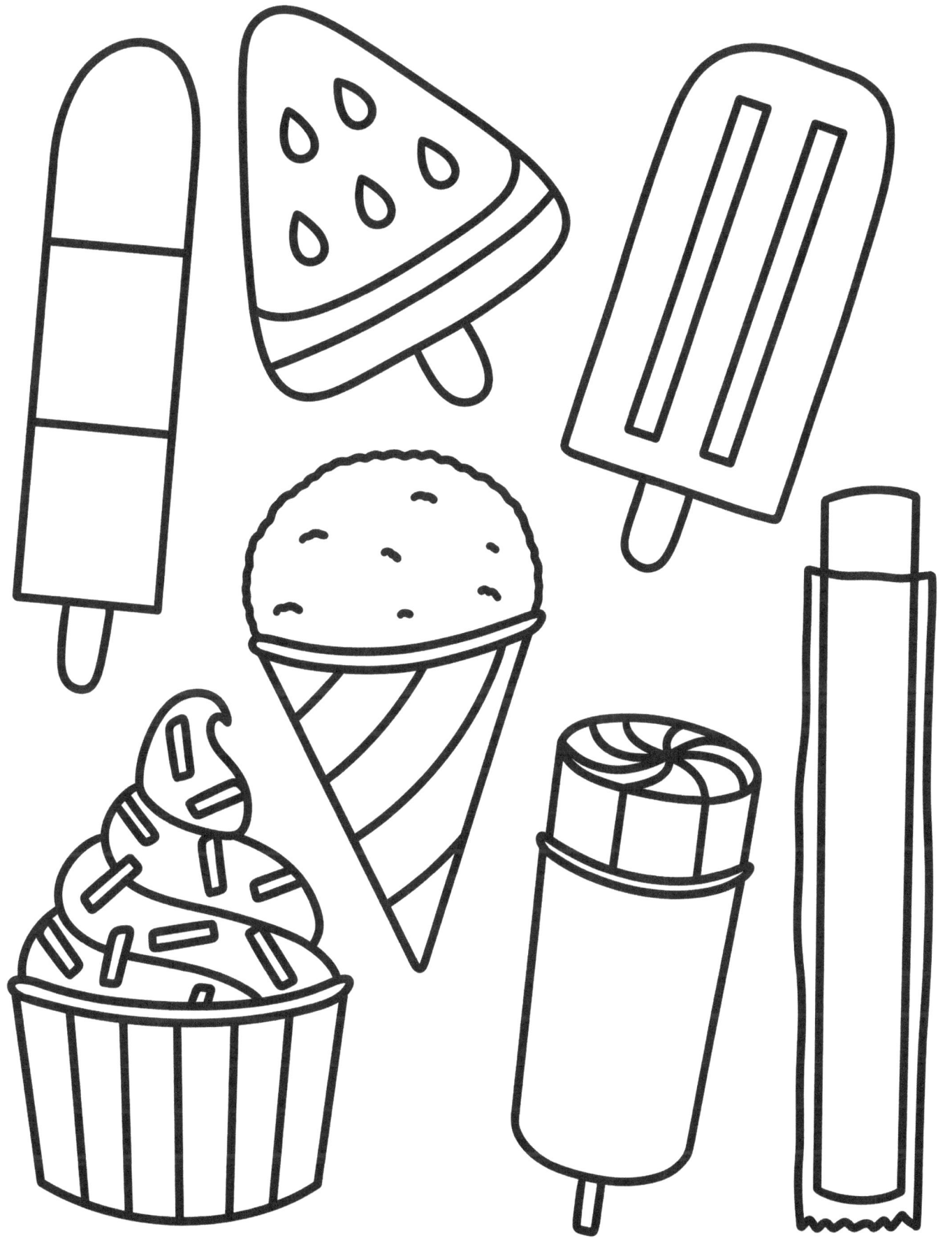

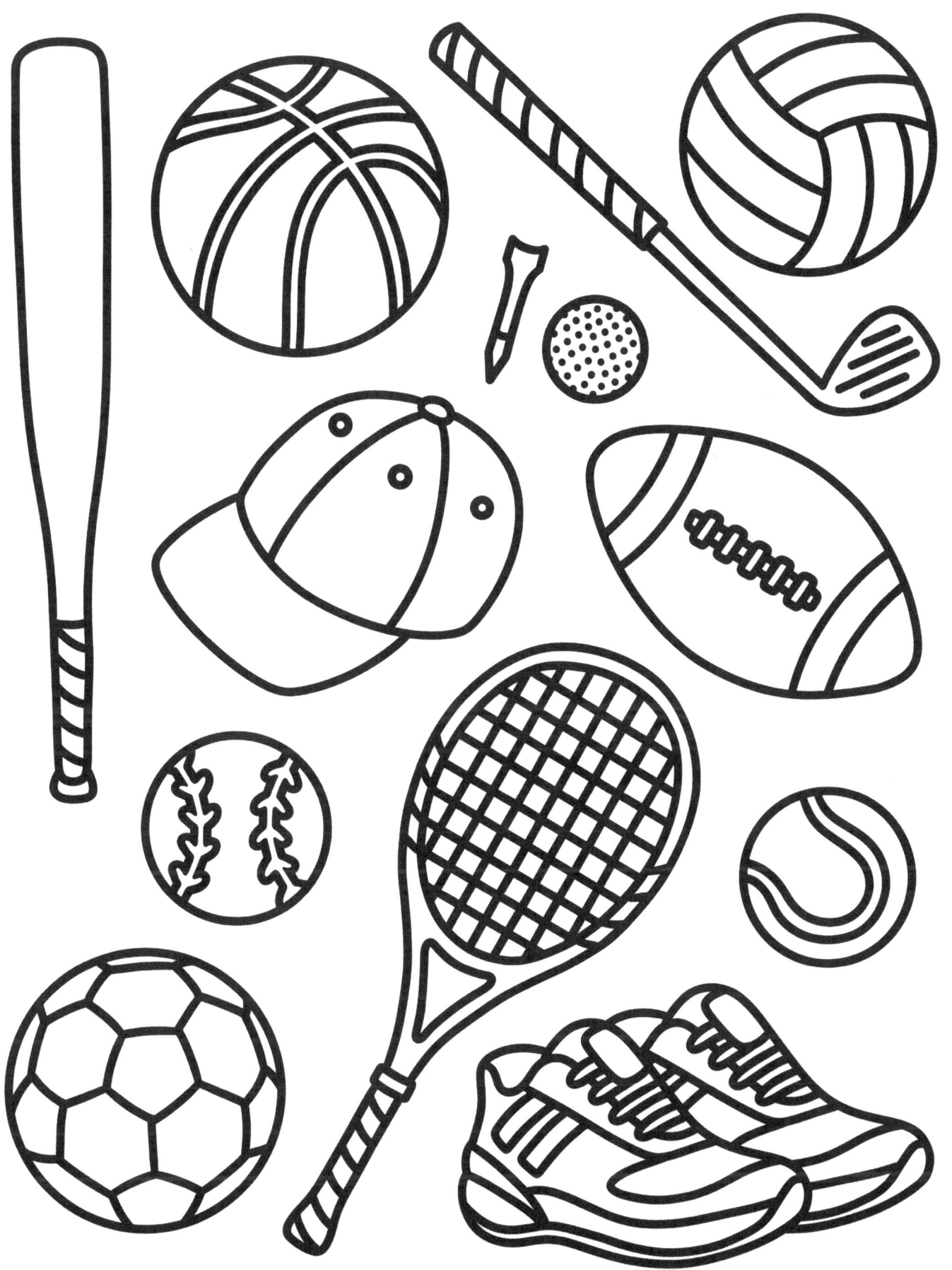

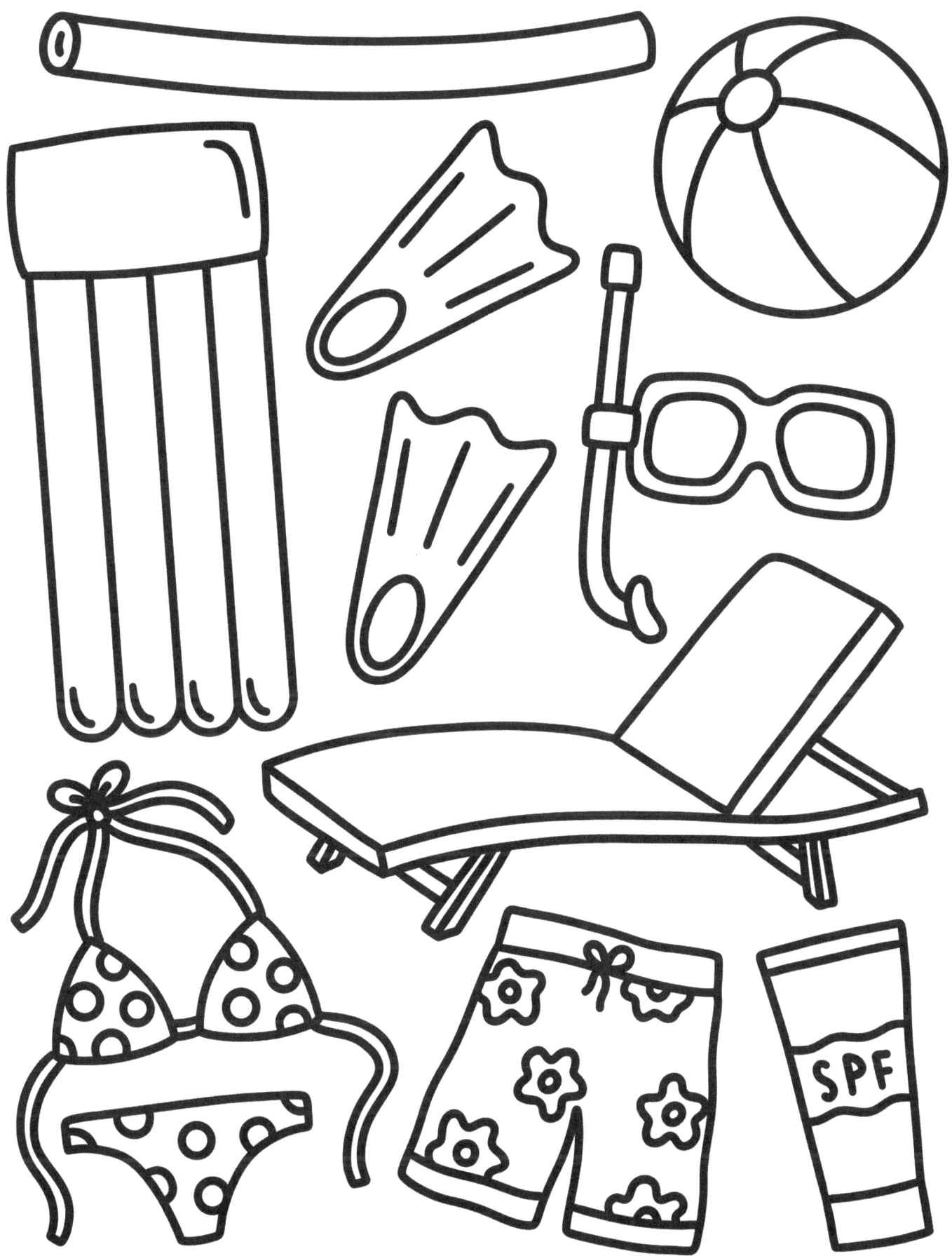

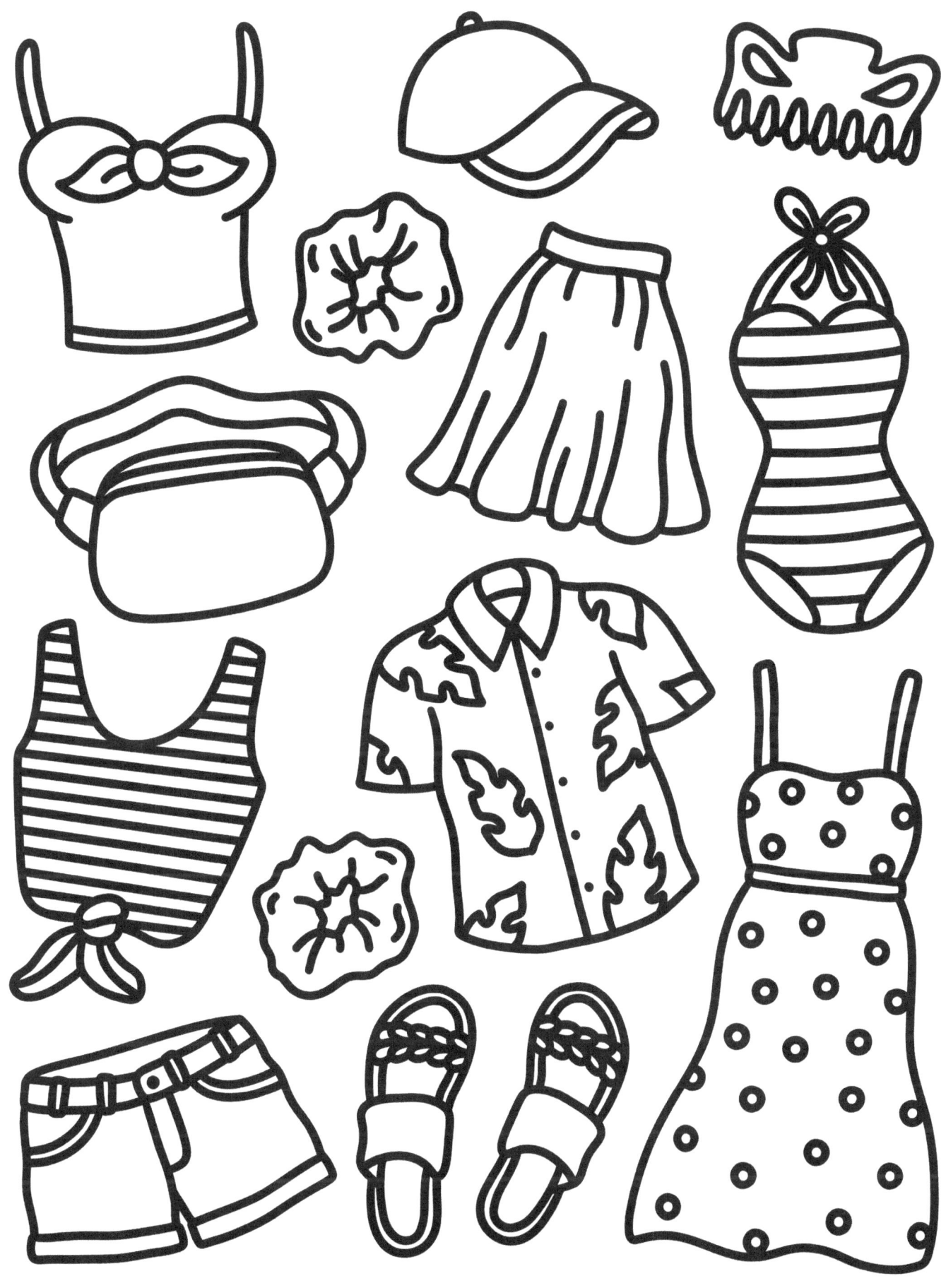

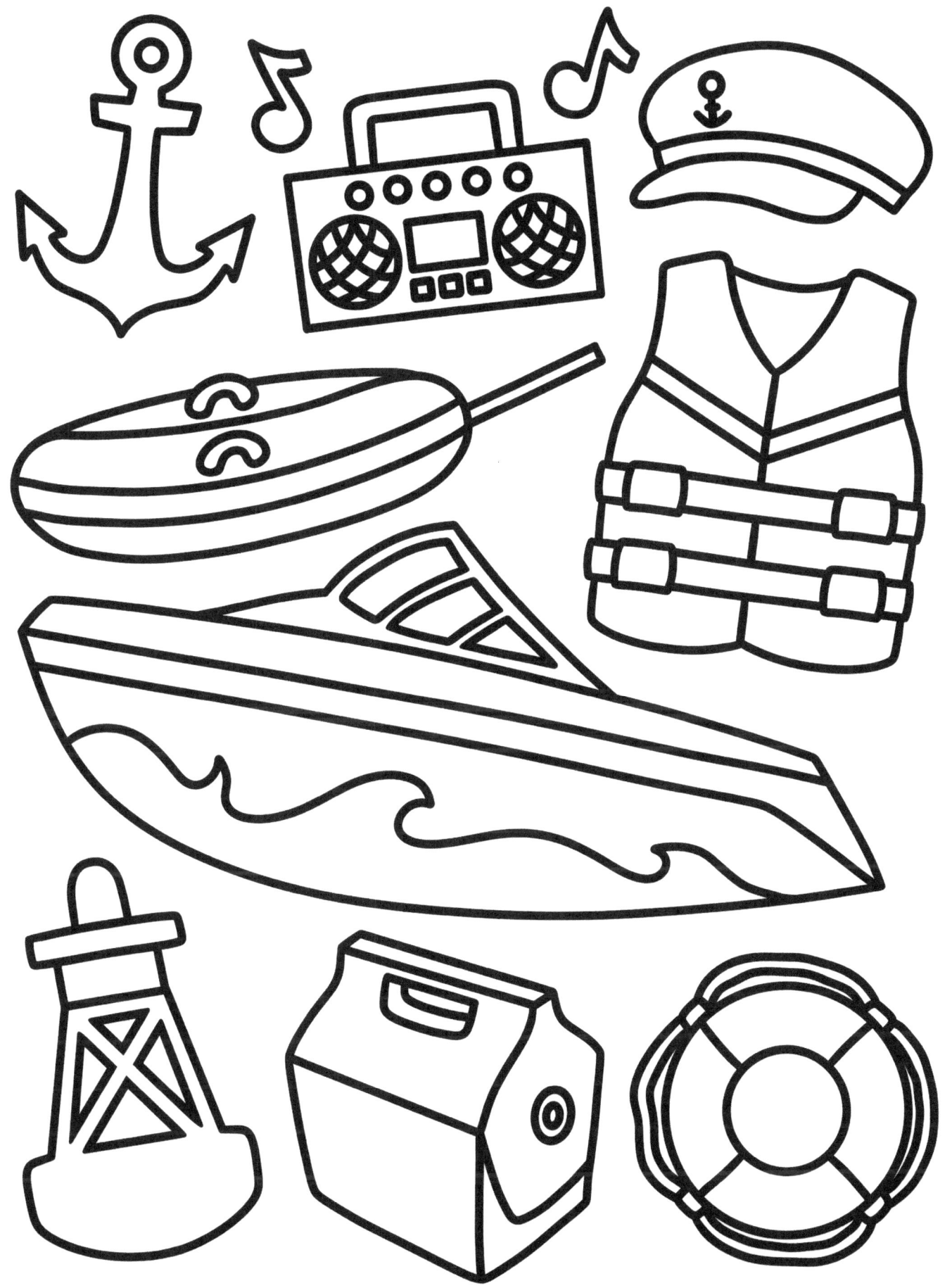

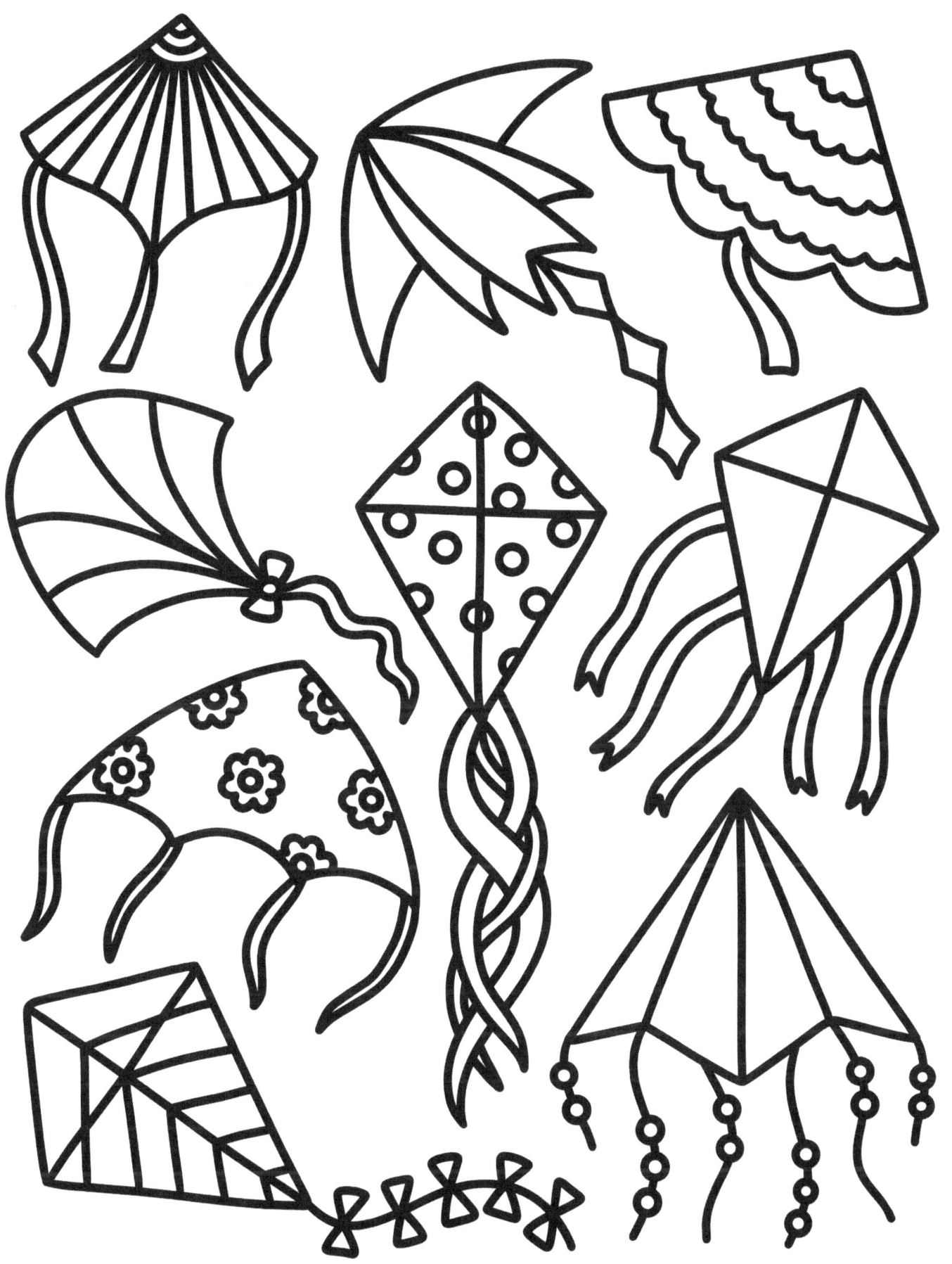

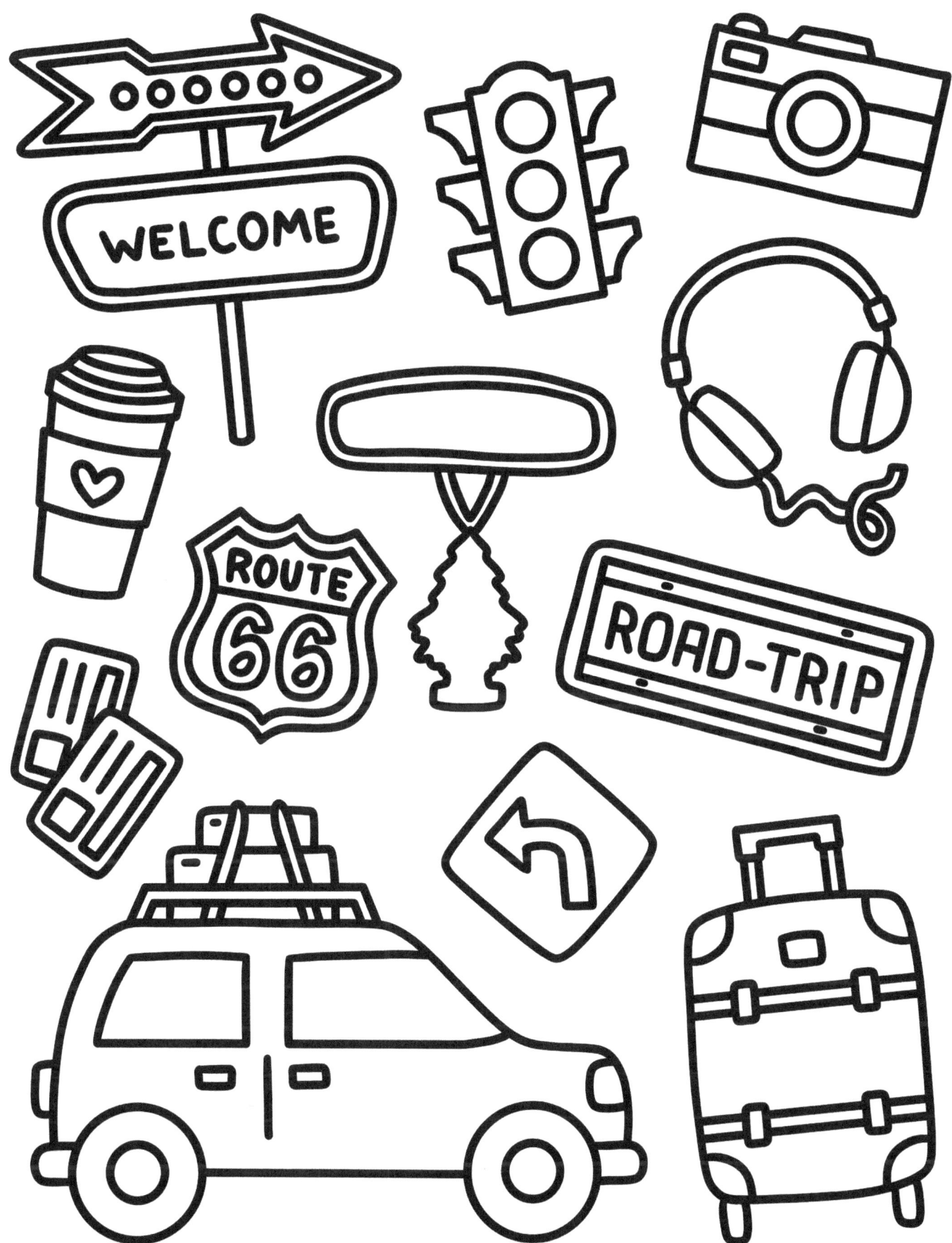

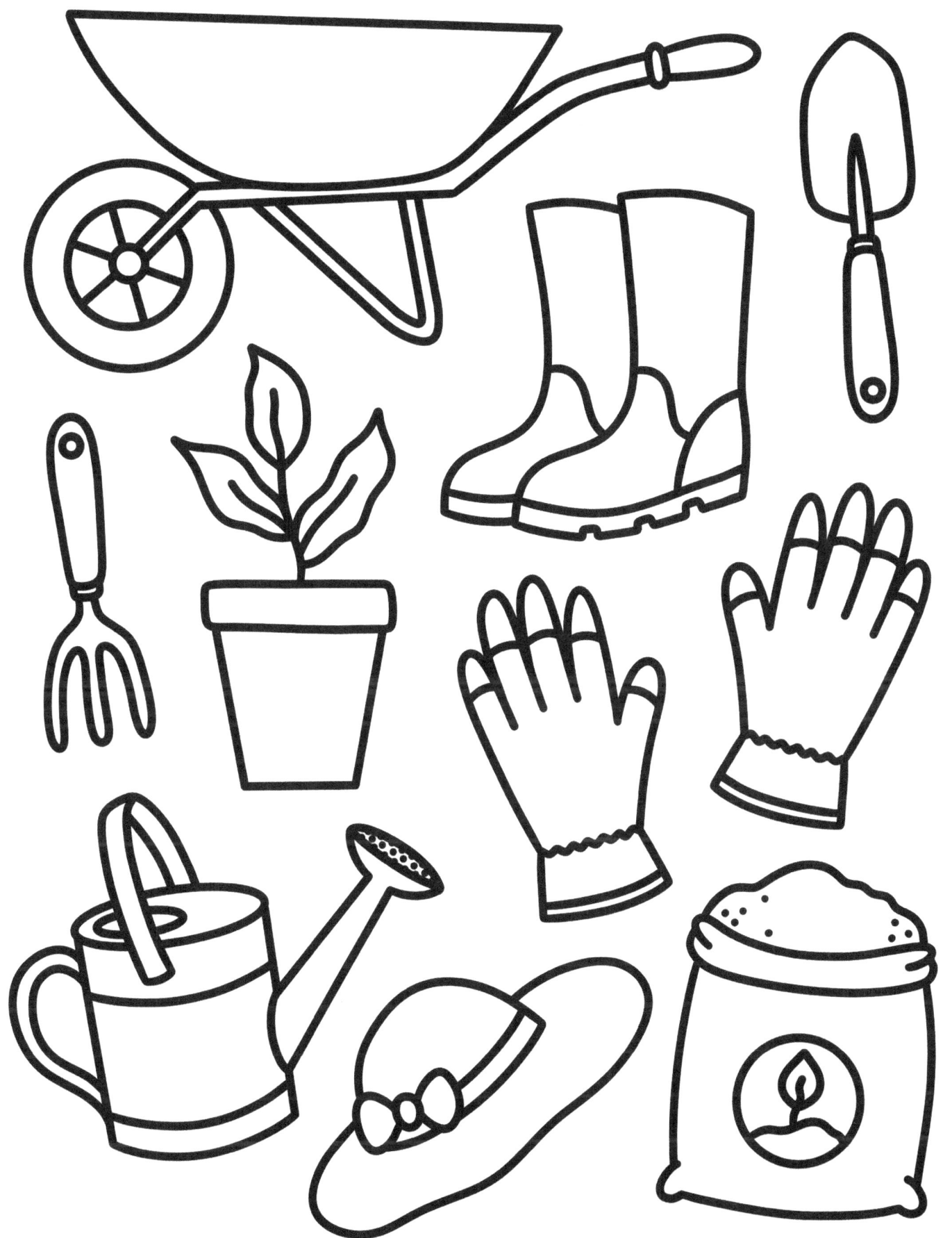

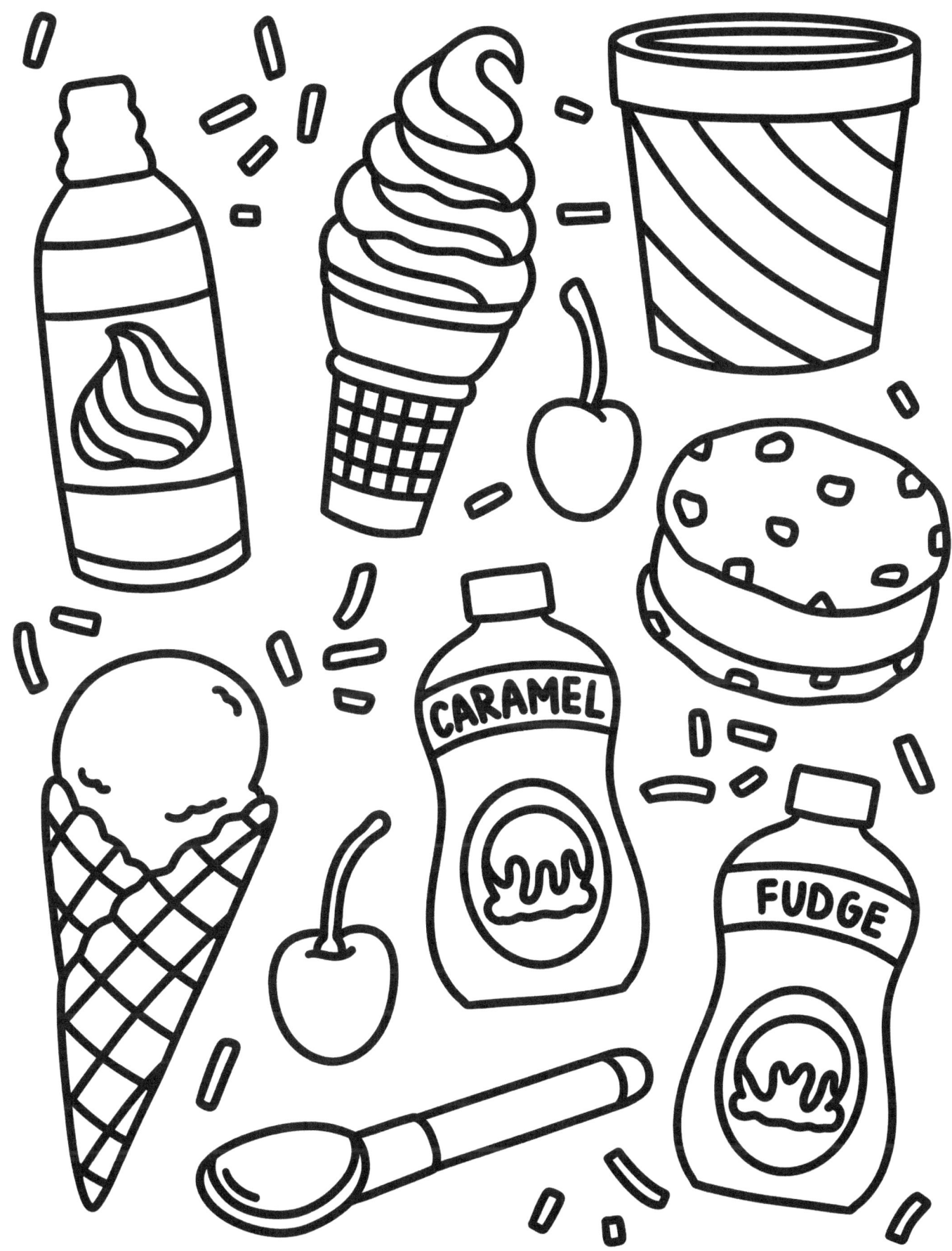

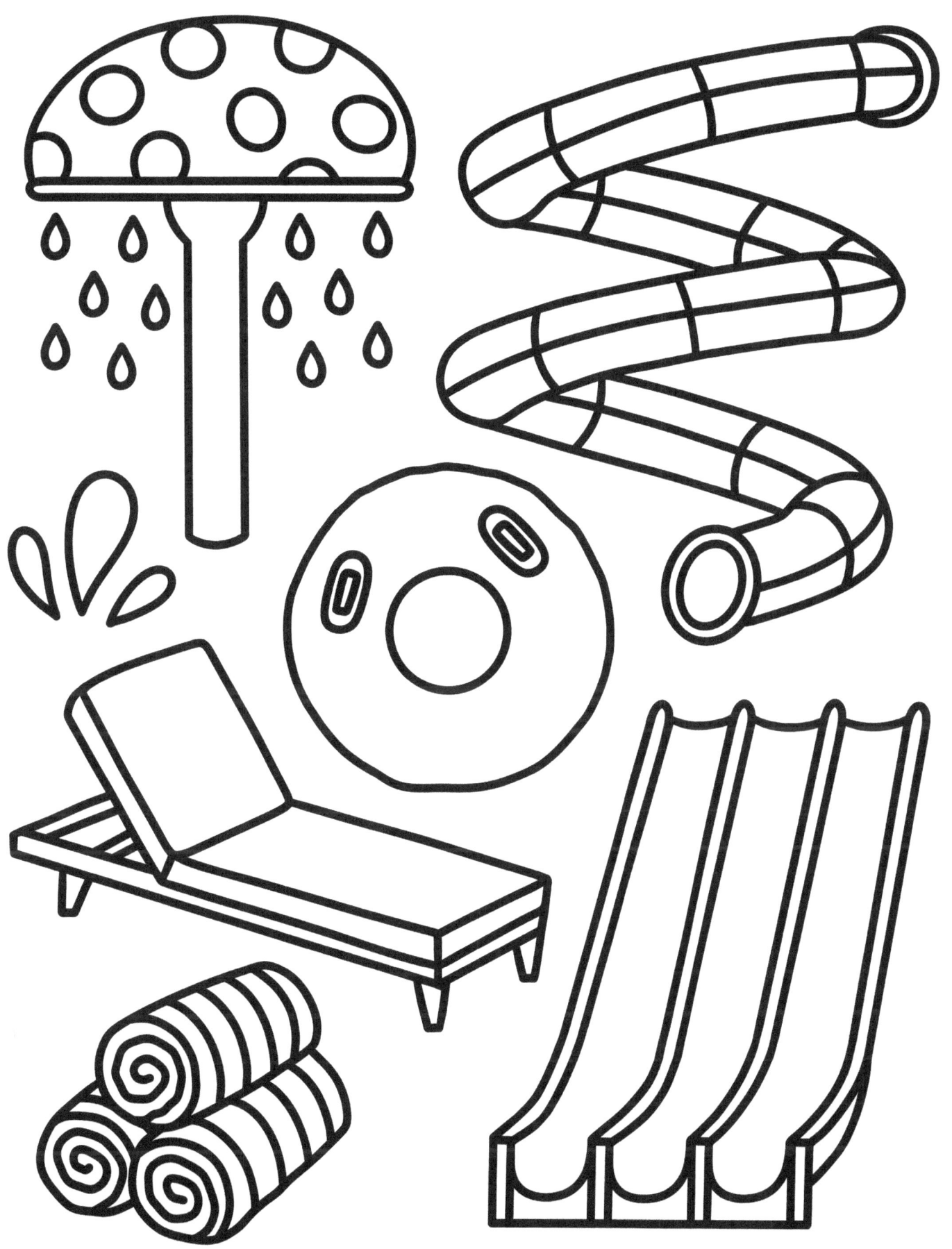

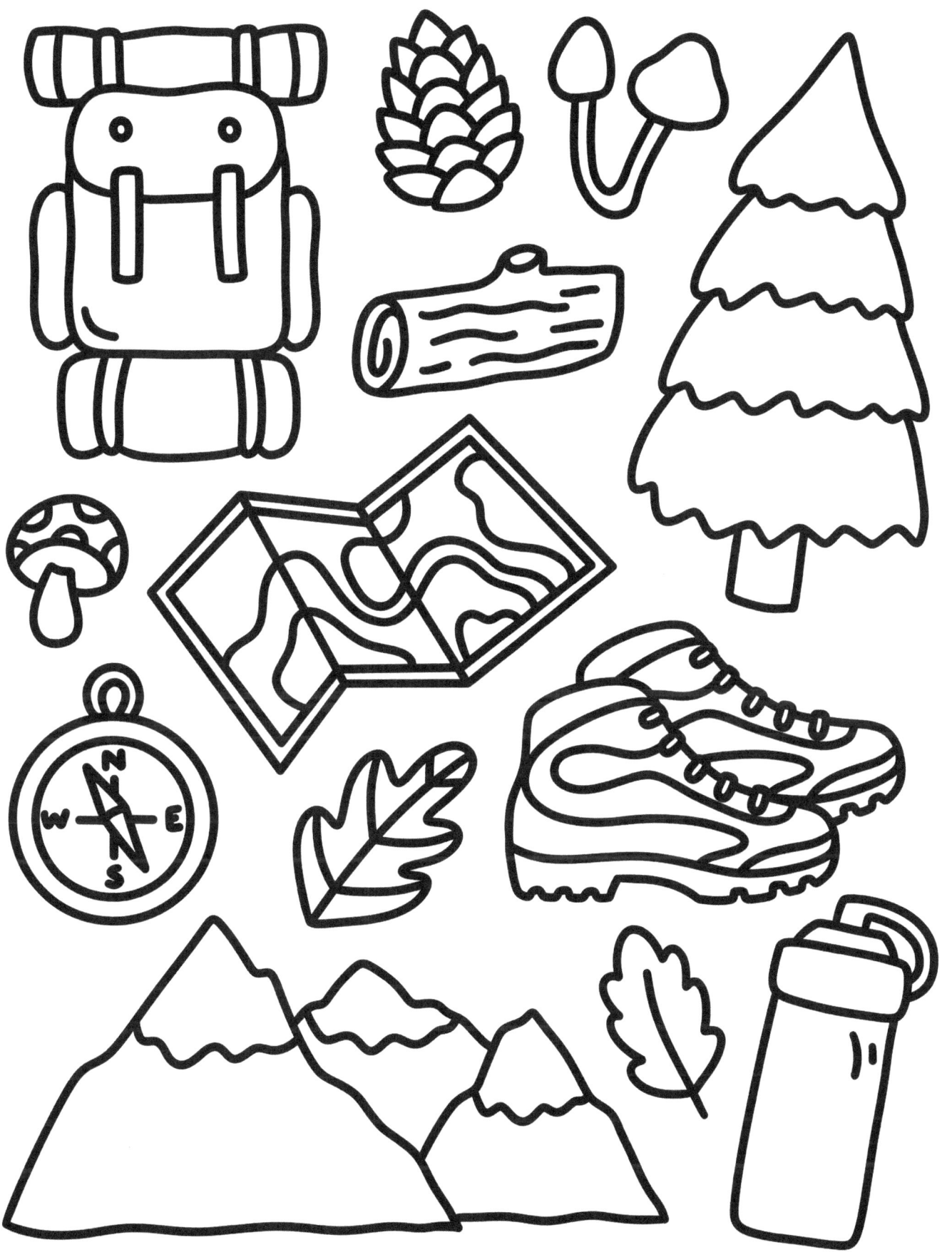

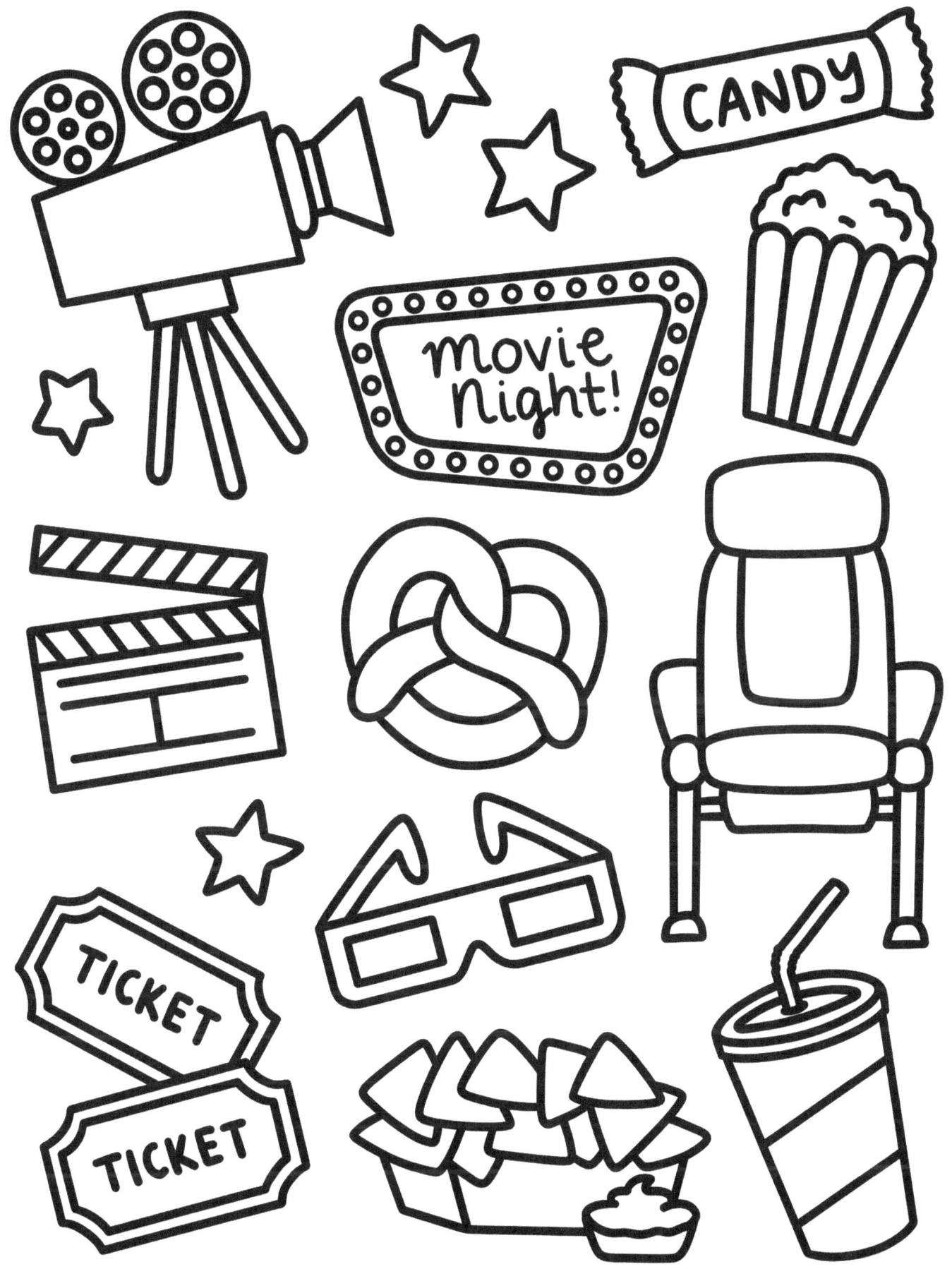

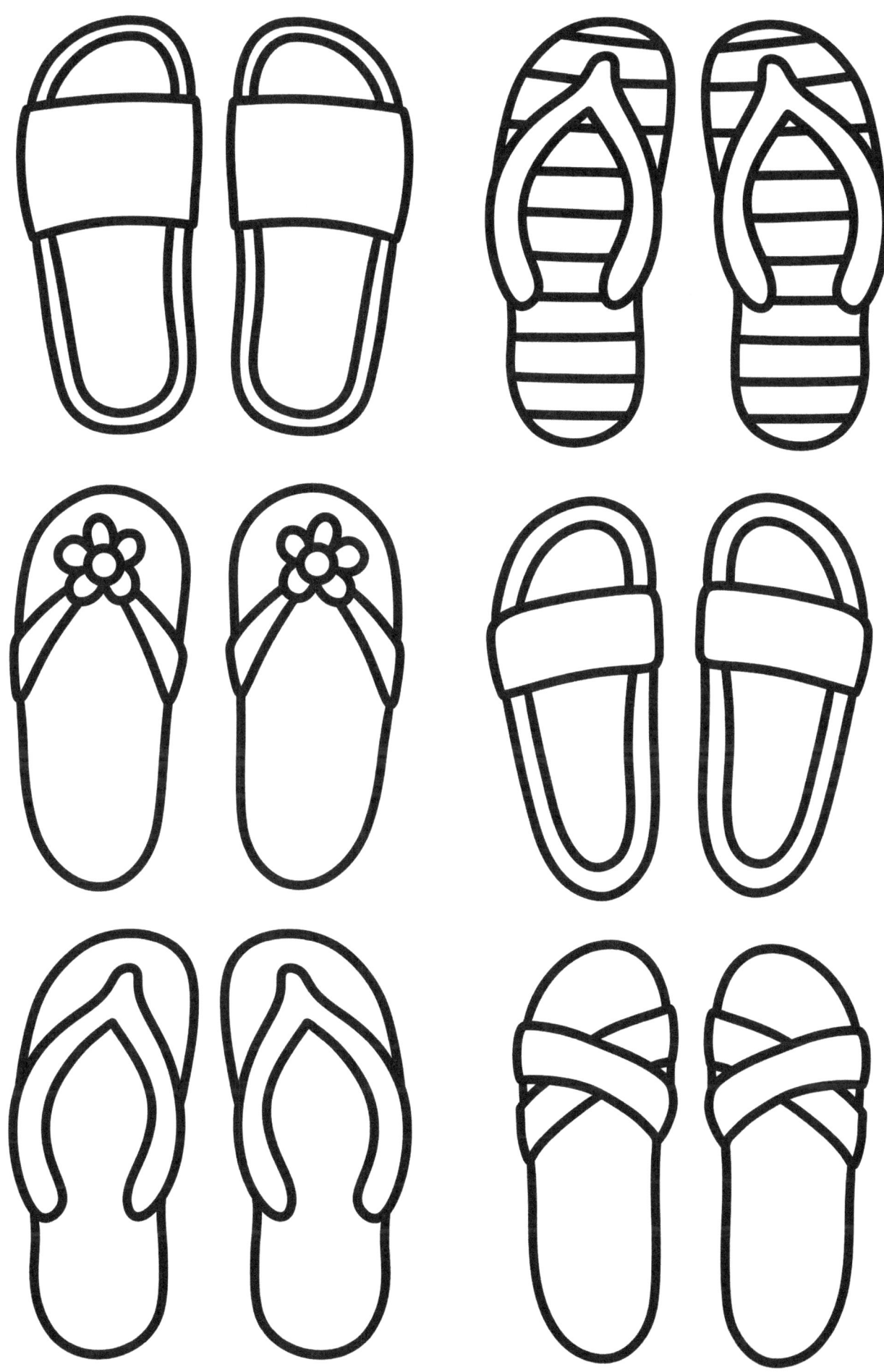

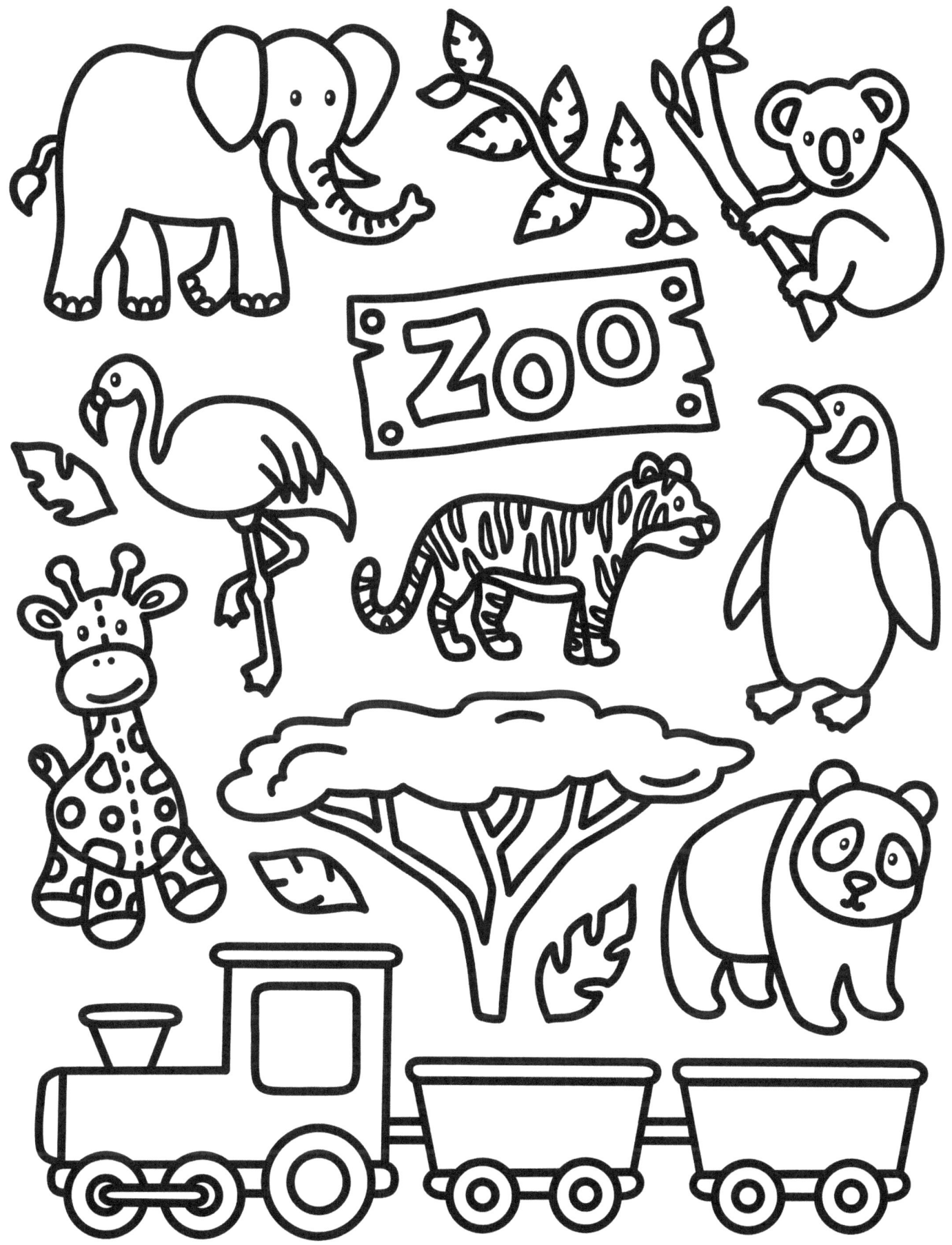

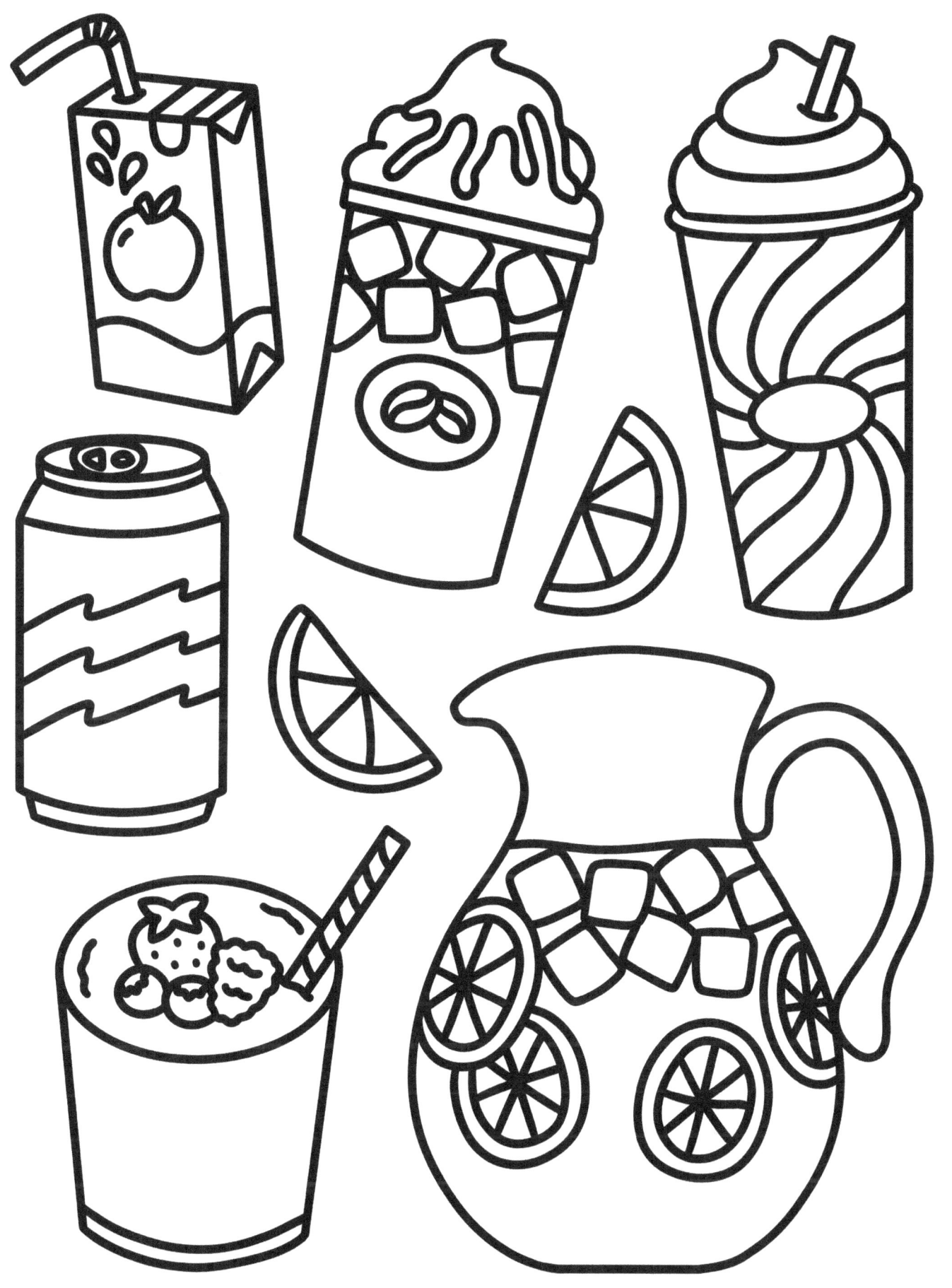

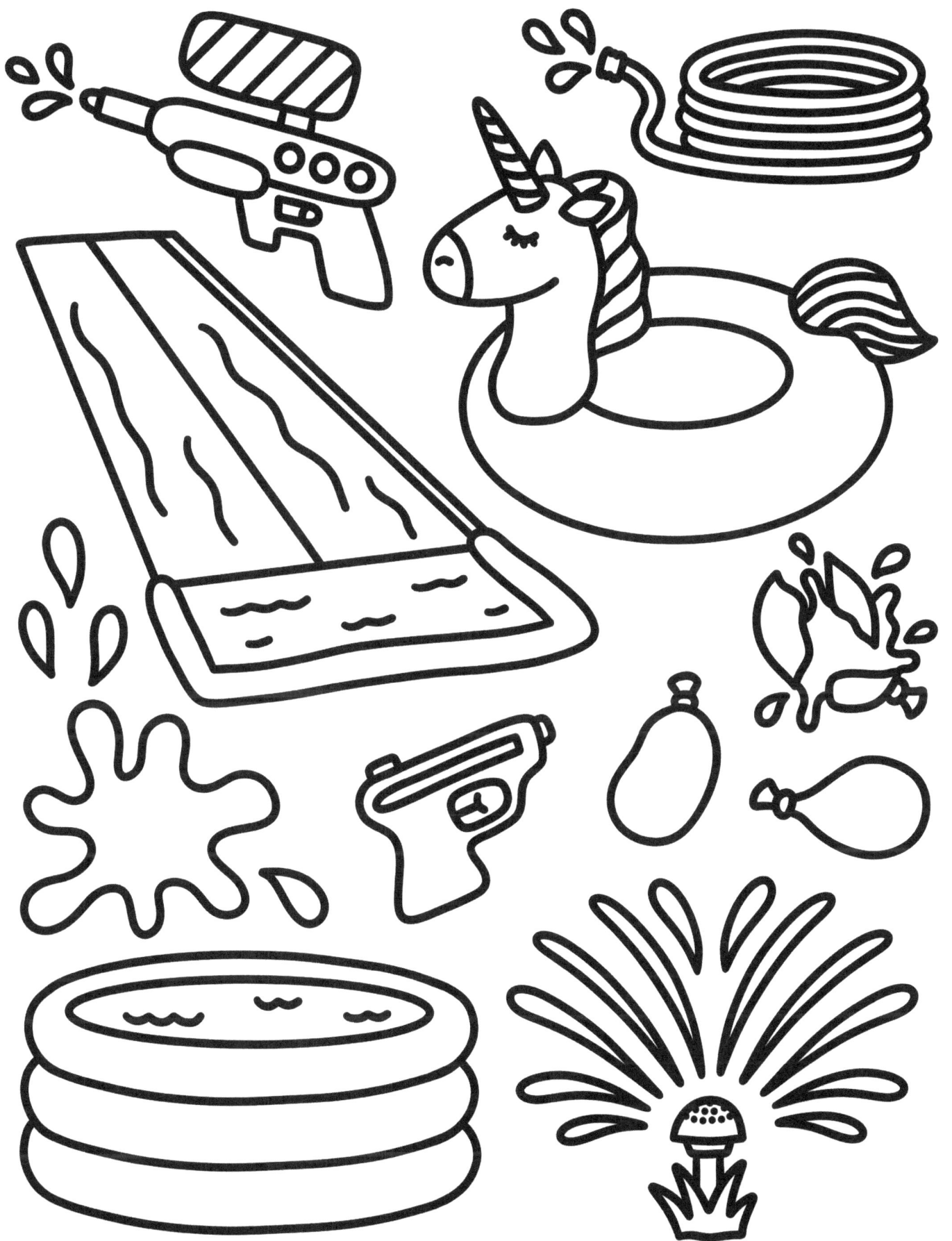

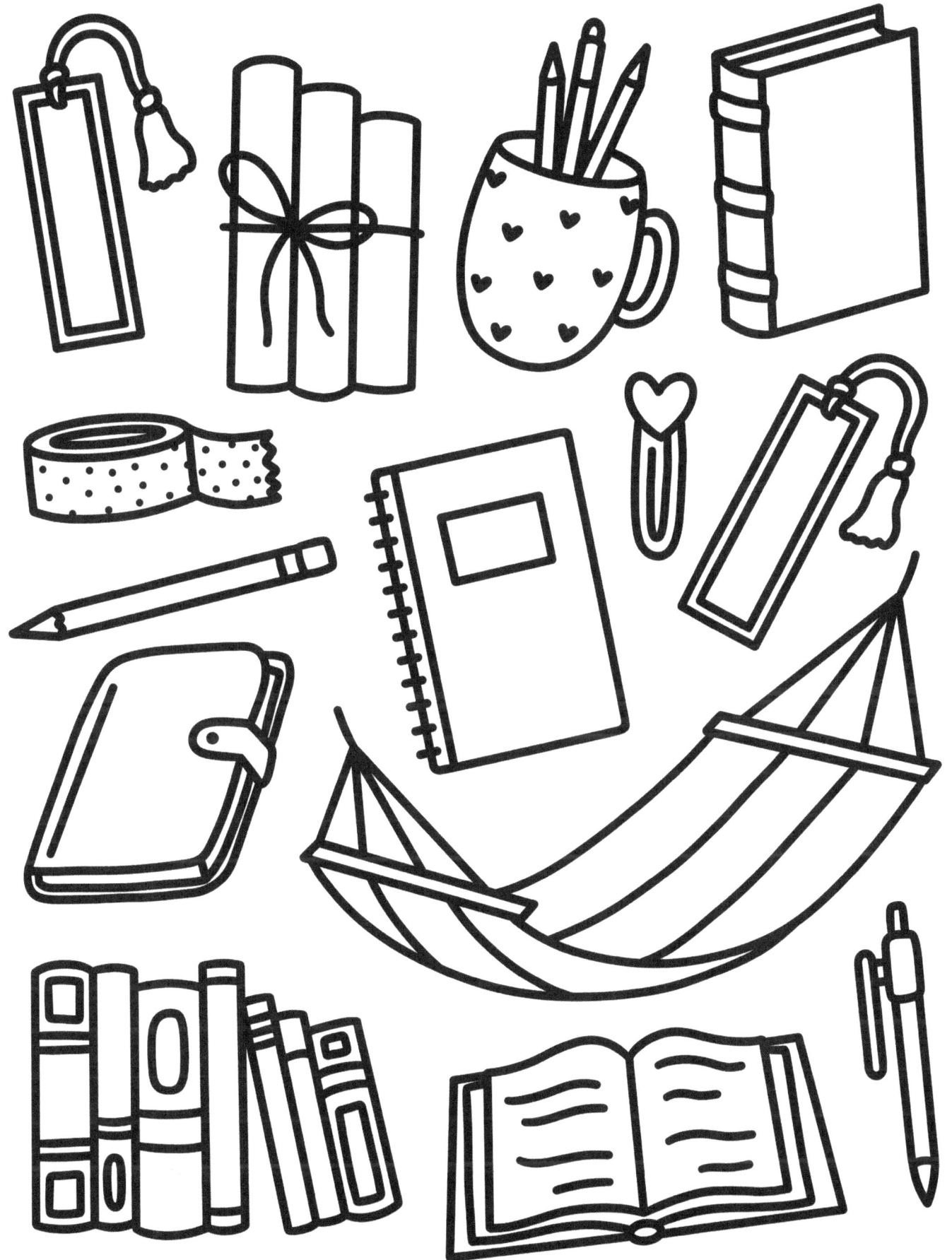

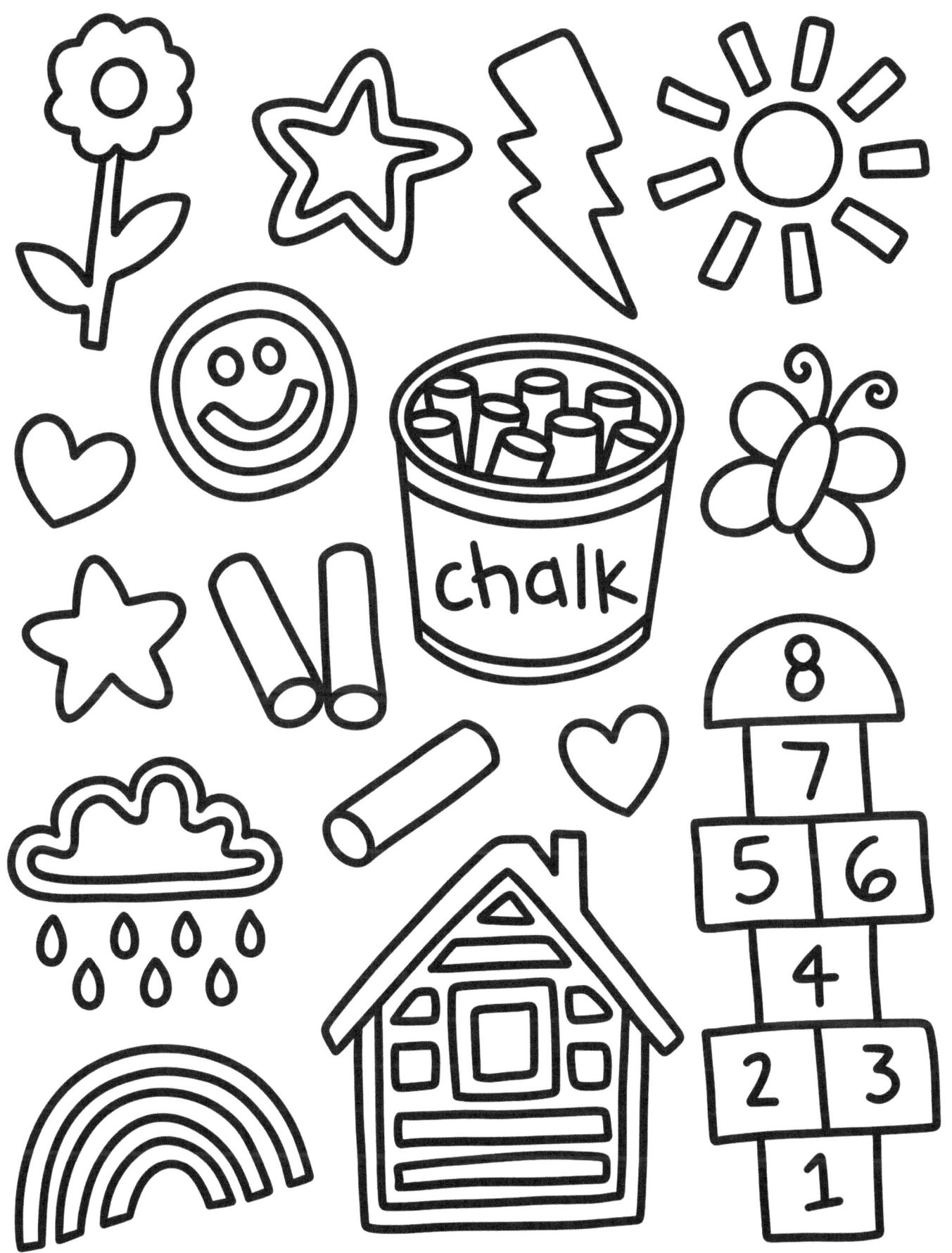

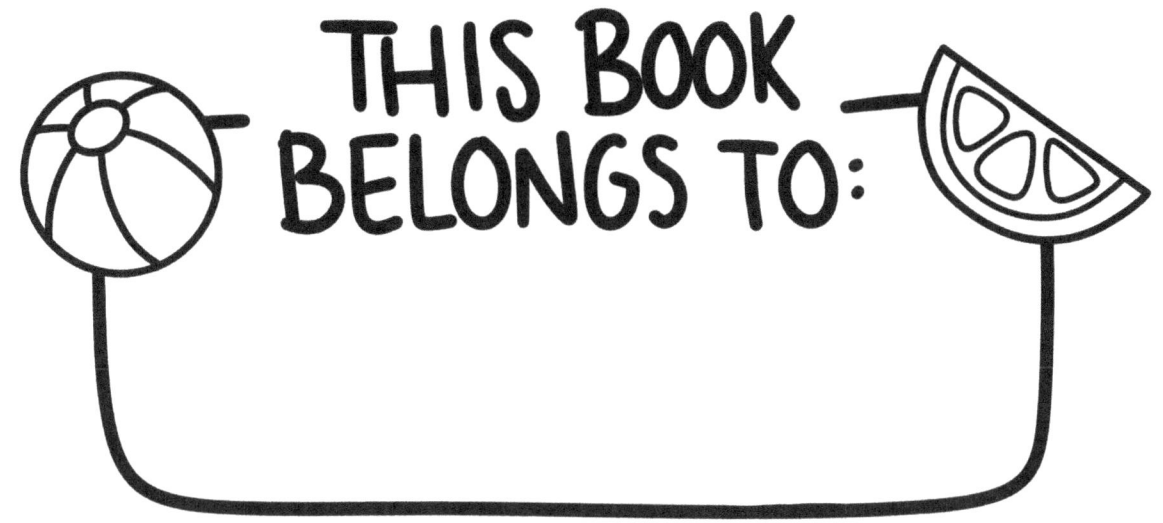

Thank you so much for purchasing one of my collage style coloring books! I hope you have as much fun coloring the designs as I did drawing them. I appreciate all the support so much!
♡ megan

MeganMilesArt.com

P.S. THE PAGES ARE SINGLE-SIDED TO PREVENT MARKER BLEED BUT YOU STILL NEED TO PUT EXTRA PAPER OR CARD STOCK UNDER IT.

Extra paper for testing markers or to put behind
the page you're coloring to prevent bleeding

Extra paper for testing markers or to put behind
the page you're coloring to prevent bleeding

Extra paper for testing markers or to put behind
the page you're coloring to prevent bleeding

Extra paper for testing markers or to put behind
the page you're coloring to prevent bleeding

www.ingramcontent.com/pod-product-compliance
Lightning Source LLC
Chambersburg PA
CBHW082359220526
45470CB00008B/2796